RECIPES
from the
VINEYARDS
of
NORTHERN
CALIFORNIA

PASTA
with Red Wine

Leslie Mansfield

CELESTIALARTS
Berkeley, California

When preparing recipes that call for egg yolks or whites, whether or not they are to be cooked, use only the highest quality, salmonella-free eggs.

CELESTIALARTS

P.O. Box 7123
Berkeley, California 94707

Distributed in Canada by Ten Speed Canada, in the United Kingdom and Europe by Airlift Books, in New Zealand by Southern Publishers Group, in Australia by Simon & Schuster Australia, in South Africa by Real Books, and in Singapore, Malaysia, Hong Kong, and Thailand by Berkeley Books.

Cover and interior design by Greene Design
Cover photograph by Larry Kunkel
Photo styling by Veronica Randall
Public Domain Art thanks to Dover Publications

Library of Congress Card Catalog Number 99-80106

First printing, 2000
Printed in the United States

1 2 3 4 5 6 7 — 03 02 01 00

To my father,

STEWART WHIPPLE,

whose guidance has helped me steer the craft.

ACKNOWLEDGMENTS

Deepest gratitude goes to my husband, Richard, who has helped me with every step—his name belongs on the title page along with mine. To my wonderful parents, Stewart and Marcia Whipple, for their unflagging confidence. To Phil Wood, who makes dreams a reality. To my dear friend and editor Veronica Randall, whose creativity, intelligence, and wit makes working with Celestial Arts a joy. To Brad Greene, for another spectacular design. To Larry Kunkel, for his glorious photography.

Finally, this book would not have been possible without the cooperation of all our friends at the wineries who graciously contributed their favorite recipes. I wish to thank them all for their generosity.

Table of Contents

Introduction

Just mention California wine country and thoughts of warm sunshine, vines heavy with ripening grapes, and a relaxed lifestyle come to mind. The small villages throughout the wine country each have their own personalities, as do the wineries. From rural, family-run boutique wineries to large stately wineries surrounded by a sea of vineyards, they all have one thing in common, a love for good food and wine.

This love of food and wine has resulted in an explosion of cutting-edge ideas that have defined California cuisine, incorporating the finest of Europe and Asia, while drawing on the incredible local and seasonal bounty.

Entertaining is a way of life in wine country. Whether it is a formal dinner with many courses to showcase a variety of wines, or just drawing off a pitcher of new wine from the barrel to go with an impromptu picnic with neighbors, the desire to share the best they have to offer has helped shape the cuisine of California.

In the following pages you will find recipes offered from the finest wineries of Northern California. Each reflects the personality of the winery it comes from, whether formal or casual, and all are delicious. Each one is a taste of wine country.

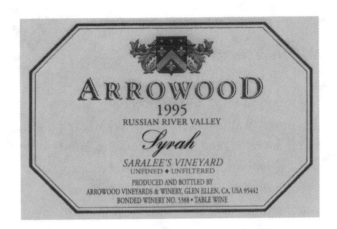

ARROWOOD VINEYARDS AND WINERY

Richard Arrowood, one of California's most renowned winemakers, along with his wife and partner Alis Demers Arrowood, have crafted a winery that sits in perfect harmony with its environs. Fashioned after a New England farmhouse, the winery has often been described as a "winemaker's dream." Maker of a number of wonderful, rare, and outstanding wines, Richard Arrowood uses his intimate knowledge of the Sonoma Valley's many microclimates and terroirs to create great and complex wines.

PASTITSIO

This is a Greek version of comfort food; baked pasta layered with lamb, cream sauce, and cheese.

2 tablespoons olive oil

1 onion, finely chopped

1 pound ground lamb

1/2 cup Arrowood Vineyards and Winery Russian River Valley Syrah

1 pound Roma tomatoes, peeled, seeded, and chopped

1 tablespoon tomato paste

1 bay leaf

1 teaspoon basil

Salt and freshly ground black pepper to taste

2 tablespoons minced fresh Italian parsley

1 pound macaroni, cooked in boiling salted water until al dente, then drained

1/4 cup melted butter

2 eggs lightly beaten

1/8 teaspoon freshly grated nutmeg

4 ounces freshly grated Kefalotryi or Parmesan cheese, divided

(recipe continued on next page)

BÉCHAMEL SAUCE:

1/4 cup butter, softened

1/4 cup all-purpose flour

2 cups milk

1/2 teaspoon salt

1/2 teaspoon white pepper

1/8 teaspoon freshly grated nutmeg

1 egg yolk

Preheat oven to 350°F. Lightly oil a 9 x 13-inch baking dish.

In a large saucepan, heat olive oil over medium heat. Add the onion and sauté until tender. Add the lamb, and sauté until lightly browned. Stir in the wine and bring to a simmer. Stir in the tomatoes, tomato paste, bay leaf, basil, salt, and pepper and bring to a simmer. Cover and reduce heat to medium-low. Simmer for 30 minutes, stirring often. Remove the cover and stir in the parsley. Continue to simmer until mixture is thick and the liquid is absorbed. Set aside.

In a large bowl, toss hot pasta with melted butter until well coated. Cool the pasta completely. In a small bowl, whisk together eggs, nutmeg, and half of the Kefalotryi cheese. Add the egg mixture to the cooled pasta and toss to coat. Set aside.

For the béchamel sauce: In a saucepan, whisk together the butter and flour until blended. Cook over medium-high heat, whisking constantly, until bubbly. Whisk in the milk and continue to whisk until mixture thickens. Remove from heat and whisk in the salt, white pepper, and nutmeg. Whisk in the egg yolk until smooth.

Spread half of the pasta in the bottom of the prepared baking dish. Spread the lamb mixture evenly over the pasta. Spread the remaining pasta mixture over the lamb. Pour the béchamel sauce evenly over the top, making sure that all of the pasta is covered. Sprinkle the remaining half of the cheese over the top. Bake for about 50 minutes, or until the top is nicely browned. Remove from oven and let cool for 10 minutes before cutting into squares.

Serves 6 to 8
Serve with Arrowood Vineyards and Winery
Russian River Valley Syrah

BEAULIEU VINEYARD

Beaulieu Vineyard (BV) was founded in 1900 by Georges de Latour, who came from a winegrowing family in Bordeaux. Since its inception, BV has been an historic, important player in the history of California winemaking. Under the guidance of legendary winemaker Andre Techelistcheff, beginning in 1938, BV's famous Georges de Latour Cabernet Sauvignon Private Reserve set the standard for California Cabernet Sauvignon through the rest of the century. Madame de Latour, who ran the company in the 1940s, was a brilliant and outspoken promoter of BV who even had the audacity to show her family's wines in her native France, and won them over. BV has been a major pioneer of the cool Carneros District of Napa, now legendary for fine Pinot Noir and Chardonnay. The winery is now owned by United Distillers & Vintners North America, and the current winemaker, Joel Aiken, continues the great tradition, along with a fine sense of innovation, established by Georges de Latour and Andre Techelistcheff.

PENNE *with* Braised Lamb & Spinach

This hearty dish cries out for a glass of Beaulieu Vineyards Cabernet Sauvignon.

1/2 cup olive oil, divided

4 lamb shanks

Salt and freshly ground black pepper to taste

1 cup chopped onion

1/4 cup chopped carrot

1/4 cup chopped celery

1 cup Beaulieu Vineyards Cabernet Sauvignon

6 cups low-sodium chicken stock

2 bay leaves

6 whole black peppercorns

2 carrots, julienned

4 ounces shiitake mushrooms, sliced

4 shallots, thinly sliced

1 tablespoon minced garlic

1 tablespoon minced fresh thyme

6 ounces baby spinach, roughly chopped

1 tablespoon butter

1 pound penne pasta, cooked in boiling salted
    water until al dente, then drained

1/2 cup freshly grated Parmesan cheese

(recipe continued on next page)

�֍ Preheat the oven to 350°F.

In a large ovenproof pot, heat 3 tablespoons of the olive oil over medium-high heat. Season the lamb with salt and pepper then add to the pot and brown well on both sides. Transfer lamb to a plate. Add 2 tablespoons of the olive oil to the pot and add the onion, carrots, and celery, and sauté until tender. Stir in the wine and simmer until the liquid is reduced by half. Return the lamb to the pot and add chicken stock, bay leaves, and peppercorns. Bring to a simmer then cover and place in the oven. Cook for about 2 hours, or until lamb is very tender. Remove from the oven and transfer lamb to a cutting board. When cool enough to handle, remove meat from the bones and chop coarsely. Strain the broth through a sieve and discard the solids. Return broth to the pot and skim off the fat. Simmer over medium-high heat until the liquid is reduced by half.

In a large skillet, heat the remaining olive oil over medium heat and add the julienned carrots. Sauté until just tender. Add the mushrooms, shallots, garlic, and thyme and sauté until the mushrooms are tender. Add the reduced lamb broth and simmer until the liquid is reduced by half. Add the spinach and simmer until wilted. Stir in the butter.

Add the lamb and hot pasta and simmer until the sauce is almost absorbed into the pasta. Divide onto 6 large shallow bowls and sprinkle with Parmesan. Serve immediately.

Serves 6
Serve with Beaulieu Vineyards
Cabernet Sauvignon

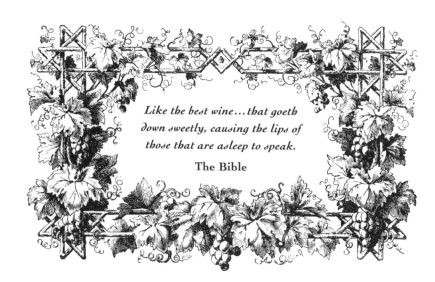

Like the best wine...that goeth down sweetly, causing the lips of those that are asleep to speak.

The Bible

BELVEDERE VINEYARDS
AND WINERY

In Italian, "belvedere" means "beautiful view," which aptly describes the vista from this rustic redwood winery in the Russian River Valley. The winery was built in 1982, which was the same year owners Bill and Sally Hambrecht bought their first piece of vineyard land high atop Bradford Mountain in Dry Creek Valley. Over the years they purchased and planted additional estate vineyards in the Dry Creek, Alexander, and Russian River Valleys in Northern Sonoma County. As Bill Hambrecht often says, "Our most valuable asset is our vineyards. Good vineyards are as valuable as gold to a winery, and Belvedere has access to some of Sonoma County's best."

BRAISED OXTAILS
with Poached Eggs
over Fettuccine

Oxtails are a delicious and inexpensive cut of meat that becomes meltingly tender after several hours of braising. Try this robust dish from English Knowles on a cold, blustery evening.

3 pounds oxtails

Salt and freshly ground black pepper to taste

2 tablespoons olive oil

1 onion, chopped

2 carrots, chopped

3 cloves garlic, minced

4 cups low-sodium beef stock

2 cups Belvedere Vineyards and Winery Dry Creek Valley Zinfandel

1 tablespoon herbes de Provence

1 bay leaf

Salt and freshly ground black pepper to taste

1 tablespoon cider vinegar

1 pound fettuccine

6 eggs

6 tablespoons chopped fresh parsley

(recipe continued on next page)

❦ Season oxtails well with salt and pepper. In a heavy Dutch oven, heat olive oil over medium-high heat. Add oxtails and brown well on both sides. Transfer oxtails to a plate. Add onion, carrots, and garlic to the Dutch oven and sauté until tender. Stir in beef stock, wine, herbes de Provence, and bay leaf. Return oxtails to the pan and cover tightly. Reduce heat to medium-low and cook for 4 to 5 hours, or until the meat is very tender. Skim off excess fat every hour. When oxtails are done, transfer to a plate and keep warm. Skim off excess fat and increase heat to medium. Simmer until sauce has reduced to about 3 cups. Remove bay leaf and season with salt and pepper to taste.

Bring a large pot of salted water to a boil. Add the fettuccine and cook until almost al dente. Drain the pasta well. Gently stir the fettuccine into the simmering sauce and continue cooking until pasta is al dente.

Bring a large skillet of water to a simmer over medium heat. Add the vinegar. Carefully add the eggs and poach until done.

Divide the fettuccine and sauce onto 6 deep plates. With a slotted spoon, carefully transfer a poached egg onto the pasta. Place 1 or 2 oxtails next to the pasta. Sprinkle with parsley and serve immediately.

Serves 6
Serve with Belvedere Vineyards and Winery
Dry Creek Valley Zinfandel

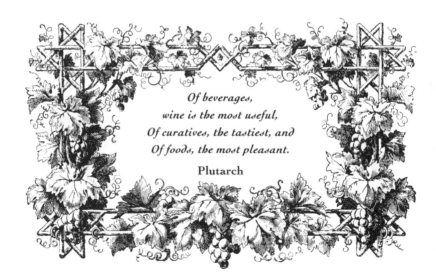

Of beverages,
wine is the most useful,
Of curatives, the tastiest, and
Of foods, the most pleasant.

Plutarch

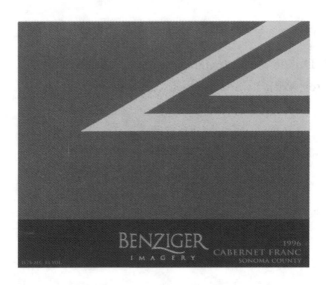

BENZIGER FAMILY WINERY

The Benziger Family, producers of Benziger Family, Reserve, and Imagery wines, believes that the nature of great wine lies in vineyard character, winemaker artistry, and family passion. At Benziger this means farming and vinifying select vineyards to mine the unique character of each, winemaking that combines intuition and artistry with a minimalist philosophy, and passion that is shared by the entire family. In its quest for uniqueness through diversity, each year the family produces over 300 lots of grapes from over 60 ranches in over a dozen appellations.

ROASTED TOMATOES
with Angel Hair Pasta

Genie Mosey came up with this bright combination of garden ingredients to showcase the Benziger Cabernet Franc.

2 pounds Roma tomatoes, cut in large dice

1 bunch scallions, sliced into 1/2-inch pieces

1 tablespoon balsamic vinegar

1 tablespoon olive oil

3 cloves garlic, minced

1 teaspoon sugar

Salt and freshly ground black pepper to taste

1 pound angel hair pasta, cooked in boiling salted
    water until al dente, then drained

1/4 cup thinly sliced fresh basil

❧ Preheat oven to 450°F. Lightly oil a 9 x 13-inch roasting pan.

Place tomatoes, scallions, balsamic vinegar, olive oil, garlic, sugar, salt, and pepper in the prepared roasting pan. Toss together until well mixed. Roast for 15 to 20 minutes. In a large serving bowl, toss hot pasta with the roasted tomato mixture and sprinkle with basil.

Serves 6
Serve with Benziger Family Winery
Cabernet Franc

BERINGER VINEYARDS

The oldest continually operating winery in the Napa Valley was started in 1876 by Jacob and Frederick Beringer, immigrants from Mainz, Germany. Currently a publicly traded company, owned by thousands of wine-loving shareholders, Beringer Vineyards excels in the production of vineyard designated reds, graceful and supple whites, and lovingly tended, botrytis-affected, late harvest dessert wines.

RABBIT BOLOGNESE
on Orecchiette with Roasted Tomatoes & Porcini Mushrooms

Beringer Vineyards' talented executive chef, Jerry Comfort, brings us this modern version of a traditional peasant's dish.

2 tablespoons vegetable oil

1 rabbit, cut into serving pieces

Salt and freshly ground black pepper to taste

2 cups veal stock

2 1/2 pounds Roma tomatoes, cut in half

10 cloves garlic

1 1/2 cups Beringer Vineyards Knights Valley Cabernet Sauvignon

1 tablespoon butter

1/4 cup chopped shallots

1 1/2 teaspoons minced garlic

8 fresh porcini mushrooms, sliced

1 1/2 tablespoons minced fresh sage

12 ounces orecchiette pasta, cooked in boiling salted water until al dente, then drained

Freshly grated Parmesan

 Preheat oven to 350°F.

In an ovenproof pot large enough to hold the rabbit in one layer, heat oil over medium-high heat.

(recipe continued on next page)

Season the rabbit with salt and pepper then brown well on all sides. Add veal stock and scrape up any browned bits. Cover pot and braise in the oven for about 1½ hours, or until very tender.

Place tomatoes and whole garlic cloves in a small baking dish and roast in oven for about 30 minutes, or until lightly browned.

In a saucepan, simmer wine over medium heat until reduced to about ½ cup. Add roasted tomatoes and garlic and simmer over medium-low heat until slightly thickened. Strain through a sieve and discard the solids. Return liquid to saucepan.

Remove rabbit from oven and transfer to a cutting board. Remove meat from bones and cut into ½-inch pieces. Add the meat and braising liquid to wine mixture. Simmer over medium-low heat until rabbit is very tender.

In a skillet, heat butter over medium heat. Add shallots and minced garlic and sauté until tender. Add mushrooms and sauté until tender. Add mushroom mixture and sage to rabbit mixture and simmer over low heat until reduced to a thick sauce.

Toss rabbit sauce with pasta and divide onto 4 plates. Sprinkle with Parmesan and serve immediately.

Serves 4
Serve with Beringer Vineyards
Knights Valley Cabernet Sauvignon

Cakebread Cellars

CARNEROS
Pinot Noir
1996

CAKEBREAD CELLARS

A true family winery, Cakebread Cellars in Rutherford is one of the most creative and successful wineries in California's famed Napa Valley. Since its founding in 1973, the winery has developed a reputation for producing world-class wines and pairing them with outstanding cuisine. Dolores Cakebread, the winery's culinary director, had the vision to plant vegetable gardens at the same time their vineyards were being planted. She has been a forerunner in the development of "California cuisine," which emphasizes fresh, natural, and locally grown produce to complement the wines of Cakebread Cellars.

RIGATONI
with Lamb & Rosemary

Lamb with a good Merlot is an ethereal match.
Try this dish on a cold winter evening.

2 pounds meaty lamb shanks

2 tablespoons olive oil

1 small onion, finely chopped

2 stalks celery, finely diced

1 carrot, finely diced

6 cloves garlic, minced

1 tablespoon minced fresh rosemary

1 cup Cakebread Cellars Merlot

4 Roma tomatoes, peeled and chopped

Salt and freshly ground black pepper to taste

$1^{1}/2$ pounds rigatoni, cooked in boiling salted water until al dente

Freshly grated Parmesan cheese

❧ Remove the meat from the lamb shanks and set aside.

Place the bones in a large saucepan and add 3 cups of water. Bring to a boil then reduce heat to medium-low and simmer for about 1 hour. Strain and reserve 2 cups of the lamb stock.

Dice the lamb into $^1/_4$-inch cubes. In a pot, heat olive oil over medium-high heat. Add lamb and sauté until browned. Add onion, celery, carrot, garlic, and rosemary and sauté until tender. Add wine and stir well to deglaze, scraping up any browned bits. Stir in tomatoes, reserved lamb stock, salt, and pepper. Cover and reduce heat to medium-low. Simmer for about 1$^1/_2$ hours to 2 hours, or until meat is very tender and sauce is thick. Toss with hot pasta and sprinkle with cheese.

Serves 6
Serve with Cakebread Cellars
Merlot

CANYON ROAD WINERY

One of Sonoma County's more picturesque settings, Canyon Road Winery is a favorite among wine country visitors. A warm and friendly tasting room features award-winning Canyon Road wines, including some limited selections available only at the winery. Enjoy a country deli and gift shop, picnic areas by the vines, complimentary wine tasting, and always great hospitality.

LINGUINE *with Salmon in Tomato Cream Sauce & Basil*

The bright flavors of the tomato cream sauce accent the fruit of the Canyon Road Pinot Noir.

3 tablespoons olive oil

3 shallots, minced

1 pound salmon fillet, skin and bones removed and cut into 1-inch cubes

2 cups heavy cream

3 tablespoons tomato paste

Salt and freshly ground black pepper to taste

1/3 cup chopped fresh basil

12 ounces linguine, cooked in boiling salted water until al dente, then drained

In a skillet, heat olive oil over medium heat. Add the shallots and sauté until tender. Add salmon and sauté until lightly browned. Stir in cream and bring to a simmer. Stir in tomato paste and simmer for about 5 minutes, or until slightly thickened. Season to taste with salt and pepper. Stir in the basil and heat through. Add the hot pasta to the skillet and toss to coat. Divide into 4 shallow bowls and serve immediately.

Serves 4
Serve with Canyon Road Winery Pinot Noir

CARDINALE WINERY

Cardinale Rule: Make grape selection an obsession and gentle winemaking a virtue. Grow fruit of intense vineyard and varietal character from the finest sites in the Mayacamas. Pick only when the fruit is physiologically ripe and balanced in flavor. Hand harvest into small lug boxes during the cool of the morning. Keep each vineyard separate, in order to know it better. Hand sort all fruit and use only sound, ripe berries. Carefully crack the berries and begin native yeast fermentation. Gently macerate juice and skins for 25 to 35 days to maximize flavor and texture. Use a traditional basket press to deepen mid-palate flavors. Place into 100% new, tight-grained French oak Chateau barrels. Attentively rack wine from barrel to barrel every three months. Age in barrel for 18 to 21 months. Bottle unfiltered. Age in bottle for 12 months before release. Enjoy or bottle age for an additional 5 to 10 years.

RICOTTA GNOCCHI
with Braised Beef Shanks

This is a rich and flavorful dinner for those cold winter nights. Cut down on last-minute prep time by making and freezing the gnocchi in advance.

BRAISED BEEF SHANKS:

3 pounds cross-cut beef shanks

Salt and freshly ground black pepper to taste

3 tablespoons olive oil

2 carrots, chopped

1 rib celery, chopped

6 cloves garlic, chopped

1 cup Cardinale Meritage

4 cups veal stock

6 sprigs fresh thyme

1 bay leaf

10 whole peppercorns

RICOTTA GNOCCHI:

$1^1/2$ pounds russet potatoes

$^1/4$ cup ricotta cheese

3 egg yolks

$^1/2$ teaspoon salt

$^1/4$ teaspoon white pepper

$^3/4$ cup all-purpose flour

(recipe continued on next page)

🌿 Make cuts through the fat around the beef shanks so they don't curl when cooking.

Season beef shanks well with salt and pepper. In a heavy Dutch oven, heat olive oil over medium-high heat. Add beef shanks and brown well on both sides. Transfer beef shanks to a plate. Add carrots, celery, and garlic to the Dutch oven and sauté until tender. Stir in wine and simmer until the liquid has almost evaporated. Stir in the veal stock, thyme, bay leaf, and peppercorns. Return beef shanks to the pan and cover tightly. Reduce heat to medium-low and cook for 2 to 2^1/2 hours, or until the meat is very tender. Skim off excess fat every hour. When beef shanks are done, transfer to cutting board and remove excess fat. Coarsely chop the meat and set aside. Pour broth through a strainer and discard the solids. Return the broth to the pot and simmer until sauce has reduced to about 1^1/2 cups. Return the reserved meat to the pot and season with salt and pepper to taste. Keep warm.

For the gnocchi: Preheat oven to 400°F.

Scrub the potatoes and prick all over with a fork. Bake for 1 hour. While the potatoes are still hot, cut in half and set aside to cool slightly. When cool enough to handle, remove the skin and discard. Put potato through a potato ricer or food mill. In a small bowl, whisk together the ricotta, egg yolks, salt, and white pepper until well blended. With a wooden spoon, stir ricotta mixture into the potatoes until well blended. Stir in the flour until you have a stiff dough. Turn out onto a lightly floured board and knead until smooth, sprinkling with additional flour if the dough sticks. Divide into 5 pieces. Using the palms of your hands, roll each piece into a log about 1 inch in diameter. Cut the logs into 1-inch pieces. Hold the gnocchi and roll along the tines of a fork to create a ridged surface. Place them on a lightly floured baking sheet so they do not touch.

Bring a large pot of salted water to a boil. Add the gnocchi and cook until they float to the surface. Transfer the gnocchi with a slotted spoon to a colander and drain well.

To serve, divide hot gnocchi into 4 shallow bowls. Spoon meat and broth over the gnocchi and serve immediately.

Serves 4
Serve with Cardinale
Meritage

**CEDAR MOUNTAIN
WINERY**

The creative interests of Linda and Earl Ault came to fruition in 1990, when they established Cedar Mountain Winery and began production of their award-winning wines. True to their belief that quality wines begin with the finest grapes in the vineyard, the Aults specialize in wines from fruit grown locally in the Livermore Valley. In addition to the classic Chardonnays and Bordelais varieties from these vineyards, a small amount of Port grown in the Sierra Foothills is also produced.

TAGLIATELLE
with Prosciutto, Eggplant,
& Tomatoes

This light meal is both easy to prepare and excellent in flavor, and if you choose a good prosciutto, you will be rewarded with a stunning taste experience.

1/2 cup olive oil

4 cloves garlic, chopped

4 ounces prosciutto, finely chopped

1 eggplant, about 1 1/2 pounds, peeled and cut into 1/2-inch cubes

2 pounds tomatoes, peeled, seeded, and chopped

1/4 cup chopped fresh basil

Salt and freshly ground black pepper to taste

1 pound tagliatelle, cooked in boiling salted water until al dente, then drained

In a skillet, heat olive oil over medium heat. Add the garlic and sauté until fragrant. Add the prosciutto and sauté until lightly browned. Add the eggplant and sauté until very tender and lightly browned. It may seem that the eggplant needs more oil since it absorbs oil so quickly. The eggplant will release the oil when it is tender. Add the

(recipe continued on next page)

tomatoes and simmer until the sauce has slightly thickened. Stir in the basil. Season to taste with salt and pepper. Toss the hot pasta with the sauce and serve immediately.

Serves 6
Serve with Cedar Mountain Winery
Merlot

When the wine goes in,
strange things come out.

Schiller

CHATEAU MONTELENA
MONTELENA
ESTABLISHED 1882

THE MONTELENA ESTATE
Cabernet Sauvignon
NAPA VALLEY
1991
GROWN, PRODUCED & ESTATE BOTTLED BY
CHATEAU MONTELENA WINERY, CALISTOGA, CALIFORNIA
ALCOHOL 14.01% BY VOLUME

CHATEAU MONTELENA
WINERY

A visit to Chateau Montelena is a must for wine lovers seeking excellence. With thick natural stone walls that maintain perfect temperature and humidity for aging wine and exceptional grapes that come from its Estate Vineyard, Chateau Montelena has earned its reputation as one of California's finest growers. For the first time in the history of winemaking, the French named the Chateau Montelena Chardonnay the world's greatest Chardonnay in 1976.

RIGATONI *with Hot Sausage & Sundried Tomatoes*

Chateau Montelena's assistant winemaker, Gerard Zanzonico, knows exactly what goes well with their fabulous wines.

3 tablespoons olive oil

2 onions, cut into slivers

3 cloves garlic, minced

4 spicy sausages, cut into $1/2$-inch slices

8 ounces zucchini, julienned

2 red bell peppers, seeded and julienned

$1/2$ cup sundried tomatoes, chopped

5 Roma tomatoes, chopped

$1/2$ cup chopped fresh basil

Salt and freshly ground black pepper to taste

12 ounces rigatoni, cooked in boiling salted water until al dente, then drained

Freshly grated Parmesan cheese

In a large skillet, heat olive oil over medium heat. Add onions and garlic and sauté until translucent. Add sausages and sauté until cooked through. Add zucchini, red bell peppers, and sundried tomatoes and sauté until just tender. Add Roma tomatoes and basil and simmer until heated through. Season with salt and pepper. Serve over hot pasta and sprinkle with Parmesan.

Serves 4
Serve with Chateau Montelena
Cabernet Sauvignon

DE LOACH VINEYARDS

The morning fog along the Russian River Valley, a product of marine influence, is instrumental for the quality of Cecil and Christine De Loach's estate grown wines. This cooling influence in the heat of late summer allows their vines to fully develop their fruit while maintaining acidity and elegance. Cecil and Christine De Loach's personal connection to their vineyards and cellar ensures a consistency of style and excellence in quality year after year.

CHICKEN BRAISED *in* ZINFANDEL *over Orzo with Corn*

The rustic "brambleberry" flavors of De Loach Zinfandel are the perfect foil to this Mediterranean accented braised chicken.

2 cups De Loach Vineyards Zinfandel

8 ribs celery, cut into 1-inch pieces

8 shallots, quartered

1 cup Kalamata olives, pitted and halved

1/2 cup capers

2 tablespoons minced fresh rosemary

2 tablespoons minced fresh sage

1/2 teaspoon salt

1/2 teaspoon freshly ground black pepper to taste

12 chicken thighs, skinned and boned

2 tablespoons olive oil

1 cup chicken stock

1/3 cup tomato paste

1 pound orzo pasta

2 cups corn kernels

(recipe continued on next page)

In a non-aluminum bowl, combine wine, celery, shallots, olives, capers, rosemary, sage, salt, and pepper. Add chicken and toss to coat. Cover the bowl, and marinate in the refrigerator 3 hours or overnight.

Preheat oven to 350°F. Oil a Dutch oven.

Remove chicken from the marinade and reserve marinade. In a large skillet, heat olive oil over medium-high heat. Add chicken and sauté until browned on both sides. Transfer chicken to the Dutch oven. Pour chicken stock into the skillet and stir up any browned bits. Whisk in tomato paste until smooth. Stir in reserved marinade and bring to a boil. Pour mixture over chicken. Cover and bake 45 minutes. Stir chicken and bake, uncovered, an additional 15 minutes.

Bring a large pot of salted water to a boil. Cook the orzo until al dente, then drain through a sieve. Return orzo to the pot and stir in corn until heated through. Divide pasta onto plates and top with braised chicken.

Serves 8
Serve with De Loach Vineyards
Zinfandel

DUCKHORN VINEYARDS

When your last name is Duckhorn, it stands to reason that you would choose a duck to be a symbol for your winery. Dan and Margaret Duckhorn have taken that theme and created one of the Napa Valley's most respected premium wineries. Hand-harvested and sorted grapes enter their crusher to emerge as ultra-premium Cabernets, Merlots, Zinfandels, and Sauvignon Blancs. New vineyards in Mendocino's Anderson Valley promise to deliver world-class Pinot Noirs to their flock of stylistic wines.

PASTA *with Fava Beans & Pancetta*

Take advantage of fava beans during their short growing season with this fresh-tasting dish.

4 pounds unshelled fresh fava beans

2 tablespoons olive oil

1 tablespoon butter

3 tablespoons minced shallots

4 ounces pancetta, finely chopped

$^{1}/_{2}$ cup water

Salt and freshly ground black pepper to taste

12 ounces spaghetti, cooked in boiling salted water until al dente, then drained

To shell the fava beans, split the pods open and strip out the beans. Bring a pot of water to a rolling boil and blanch the beans for 1 minute. Drain, then refresh in ice water. When they are cool enough to handle, drain and squeeze the beans out of their skins. Discard the skins and set aside the beans.

In a skillet, heat the olive oil and butter over medium heat. Add the shallots and sauté until tender. Add the pancetta and sauté until crisp. Pour in the water and add the reserved fava beans. Cover and simmer about 10 minutes, or until tender. Season with salt and pepper. Uncover and add the hot pasta. Stir gently until the liquid is absorbed.

Serves 4
Serve with Duckhorn Vineyards
Estate Grown Merlot

*A meal without wine
is like a day without sunshine.*
Brillat-Savarin

DRY CREEK VINEYARD

Dry Creek Vineyard was the first new winery to be established in the Dry Creek Valley of Sonoma after Prohibition. Synonymous with fine winemaking, Dry Creek Vineyard draws upon over 35 different vineyards to produce their wines, matching the particular soils and microclimates of each site to the varieties that do best.

PASTA *with Pancetta & Four Cheeses*

This rich pasta dish goes together in less than 30 minutes.

4 ounces pancetta, finely chopped

1 cup half-and-half

3 ounces fontina cheese, diced

3 ounces Gorgonzola cheese, crumbled

3 ounces Gruyère cheese, crumbled

$1/2$ teaspoon white pepper

2 ounces freshly grated Parmesan cheese

1 pound macaroni, cooked in boiling salted water
until al dente, then drained

Minced Italian parsley for garnish

In a nonstick skillet, sauté the pancetta over medium heat until crisp. Add the half-and-half and bring to a simmer. Reduce heat to low and add the fontina, Gorgonzola, and Gruyère. Cook, stirring often, until cheeses are melted. Stir in the white pepper. Stir in the Parmesan and cook until heated through. Stir in the hot pasta until well coated. Transfer to a serving bowl and sprinkle with parsley. Serve immediately.

> *Serves 6*
> *Serve with Dry Creek Vineyard Merlot*

FERRARI-CARANO
VINEYARDS AND WINERY

Villa Fiore, or "House of Flowers," at Ferrari-Carano is one of the most spectacular wineries and visitor centers in the northern California wine country. Designed to reflect the proud Italian heritage of the Carano family, Villa Fiore houses state-of-the-art kitchens, which are used to educate professionals as well as consumers in the enjoyment of Ferrari-Carano wines.

Ferrari-Carano draws its grapes from fourteen winery-owned vineyards over a fifty-mile area from Alexander Valley in the north to the Carneros district in the south. This exceptional supply of fruit allows the winemaker to produce the highly stylized wines for which Ferrari-Carano is known.

PENNE *with* Wild Mushroom Broth

Whenever you are going to reduce chicken stock, make sure that it is low in sodium so that it won't be too salty after it is reduced.

1 1/2 tablespoons butter

2 shallots, minced

4 ounces shiitake mushrooms, stems reserved and caps sliced

4 cups chicken stock, preferably homemade

4 ounces button mushrooms, sliced

4 ounces oyster mushrooms, sliced

Salt and freshly ground black pepper to taste

12 ounces penne pasta, cooked in boiling salted water until al dente, then drained

1/2 cup thinly sliced fresh basil

2 tablespoons chopped fresh Italian parsley

In a saucepan, heat butter over medium heat. Add the shallots and sauté until translucent. Add the reserved shiitake mushroom stems and sauté until lightly browned. Add the chicken stock and bring to a simmer over medium heat. Simmer until liquid is reduced to 1 cup. Strain through a fine

(recipe continued on next page)

sieve and discard the solids. Return the broth to the saucepan and add the sliced shiitake caps, button mushrooms, and oyster mushrooms. Season to taste with salt and pepper. Bring to a simmer over medium heat and simmer until mushrooms are cooked.

Place hot pasta in a large shallow serving bowl. Pour the mushrooms and broth over the pasta. Top with basil and parsley.

Serves 4
Serve with Ferrari-Carano Vineyards and Winery
Siena

FREEMARK ABBEY

The history of winemaking at Freemark Abbey stretches back to 1886, when the newly widowed Josephine Marlin Tychson made wine from the vineyards she and her deceased husband had planted. In so doing, she became the first woman in California to operate a winery. A succession of owners followed until 1939, when the winery was reopened after being closed during Prohibition. Currently Ted Edwards is managing partner and winemaker, and the winery produces all the classic Napa varieties, including a luscious late-harvest Riesling known as "Edelwein Gold."

PENNE PASTA
with Duck Ragù

The talented Shannon Kelly of Knickerbocker's Catering took our favorite fowl and created this exquisite autumn meal.

1/4 cup olive oil

2 ounces pancetta, diced

1 small onion, finely chopped

2 ribs celery, finely diced

1 carrot, finely diced

1 pound tomatoes, peeled and chopped

1 cup white wine

1/4 cup finely chopped Italian parsley

1 tablespoon fennel seed

Salt and freshly ground black pepper to taste

2 duck legs with thighs, reserve breasts for
    another use

1 1/2 pounds penne pasta, cooked in boiling salted
    water until al dente, then drained

Freshly grated Parmesan cheese

In a large pot, heat olive oil over medium heat. Add pancetta, onion, celery, and carrots and sauté until tender. Stir in tomatoes, wine, parsley, fennel, salt, and pepper. Separate the duck legs from the thighs and add to pot. Cover pot, reduce heat to medium-low, and simmer for about 1 hour or until the duck meat falls off of the bones.

Remove the duck, pull off the meat, and discard the bones and skin. Chop the meat finely and return to the pot. Skim off excess fat from the sauce and adjust seasonings. Add the hot, drained pasta to the pot and toss with the sauce. Serve sprinkled with Parmesan cheese.

Serves 6
Serve with Freemark Abbey
Merlot

GEYSER PEAK WINERY

Located just north of Healdsburg, 100-year-old Geyser Peak Winery's tradition of excellence shows in its being named "1998 Winery of the Year" by Wine & Spirits Magazine and the San Francisco International Wine Competition. The original vine covered stone winery is now the cornerstone of a state-of-the-art complex that is one of the most well equipped wineries in California. Within the winery, president and head winemaker, Daryl Groom, oversees the vinification of not only their sought-after reserve wines but also a multitude of great wines for all occasions.

ROASTED EGGPLANT LASAGNA
with Herbed Ricotta Filling & Spicy Tomato Glaze

Serve this satisfying dish with a simple salad of fresh greens dressed with a light vinaigrette.

1 pound eggplant
Olive oil

HERBED RICOTTA FILLING:

15 ounces ricotta cheese
4 ounces mozzarella cheese, grated
1/4 cup freshly grated Parmesan cheese
3 egg yolks
1 tablespoon minced parsley
1 green onion, minced
1 clove garlic, minced
1/2 teaspoon salt
1/2 teaspoon freshly ground black pepper to taste

SPICY TOMATO GLAZE:

1 tablespoon olive oil
1 clove garlic
1 can (15-ounces) tomato sauce
1 teaspoon oregano
1/2 teaspoon dried red chile flakes

12 ounces lasagna pasta
2 ounces mozzarella cheese, grated

(recipe continued on next page)   **49**

🍂 Preheat oven to 450°F. Lightly oil a baking sheet.

Trim off top and bottom of the eggplant and discard. Slice eggplant crosswise into 1/2-inch slices. Brush with olive oil and place on baking sheet. Roast for about 20 minutes, or until well browned and tender.

For the filling: In a bowl, stir together ricotta, mozzarella, Parmesan, egg yolks, parsley, green onion, garlic, salt, and pepper until well blended. Set aside.

For the tomato glaze: In a saucepan, heat oil over medium heat. Add garlic and sauté until fragrant. Add tomato sauce, oregano, and chile flakes. Bring to a simmer, reduce heat to medium-low, and cook until slightly thickened, about 15 minutes. Set aside.

Bring a large pot of salted water to a boil. Add the lasagna to the water and cook for about 8 minutes. Do not overcook or the pasta will be difficult to handle. Drain well.

Reduce oven temperature to 350°F. Lightly oil a 9 x 13-inch baking dish.

Layer half of the lasagna sheets in the bottom of the prepared baking dish, overlapping slices to cover bottom completely. Spread half of the ricotta filling evenly over the pasta. Cover filling with eggplant slices. Spread remaining filling over the eggplant. Layer remaining pasta over the filling.

Pour glaze evenly over the pasta and sprinkle with mozzarella. Bake for 35 to 40 minutes, or until heated through and bubbly.

Serves 6
Serve with Geyser Peak Winery
Shiraz

**Fill high the bowl
with Samian wine!**

Byron

GLEN ELLEN WINERY

Glen Ellen Winery was created in 1983 by the Benziger family with the idea of producing inexpensive and delicious varietal wines for an increasing number of wine consumers. Thus was born the whole category of "fighting varietals." The winery is located in Sonoma, California, with a wonderful Visitor Center located in the charming town of Glen Ellen in the historic Valley of the Moon, Sonoma County. In 1994, the Benzigers sold the winery to United Distillers and Vintners (UDV). UDV continues to produce Glen Ellen Proprietor's Reserve wines with the same degree of dedication to quality; not surprising, as the winemaking team has virtually remained the same for nearly a decade. Glen Ellen utilizes an innovative program, the Grower Feedback Loop, to encourage their many growers to improve the quality of the fruit produced each year to meet consumers' growing sophistication.

PASTA ITALIANO
with Chicken

This quintessential peasant dish would be a great Sunday dinner. Serve steaming hot with a fresh salad with balsamic vinegar and extra virgin olive oil.

¹/4 cup olive oil

6 large chicken thighs

Salt and freshly ground black pepper to taste

¹/2 cup minced onion

3 cloves garlic, minced

12 ounces tomatoes, peeled, seeded, and chopped

1 can (15-ounces) tomato sauce

3 tablespoons tomato paste

¹/4 cup minced fresh basil

¹/4 cup minced Italian parsley

1 pound spaghetti, cooked in boiling salted water
    until al dente, then drained

Freshly grated Romano cheese

In a pot, heat the olive oil over medium heat. Season the chicken with salt and pepper and add to the pot. Brown the chicken well on both sides. Cover the pot, reduce heat to medium-low, and

(recipe continued on next page)

cook for 10 minutes. Add the onion and garlic, cover, and cook for an additional 15 minutes. Stir in the tomatoes, tomato sauce, tomato paste, basil, and parsley. Cover and simmer for 45 minutes. Season to taste with salt and pepper. Divide hot pasta between 6 plates, top with a piece of chicken and spoon over the sauce. Sprinkle with Romano and serve immediately.

Serves 6
Serve with Glen Ellen Winery
Zinfandel

*To be crushed
in the winepress of passion.*
Gabriel Biel

GRGICH HILLS

Napa Valley
FUMÉ BLANC
Dry Sauvignon Blanc
1996

PRODUCED AND BOTTLED BY GRGICH HILLS CELLAR
RUTHERFORD, CA · ALC. 12.8% BY VOL. · CONTAINS SULFITES

GRGICH HILLS CELLAR

Grgich Hills Cellar, a collaboration between Miljenko Grgich and Austin Hills of the Hills Bros. Coffee family has become known as a producer of big, mouth-filling Chardonnays, which connoisseurs consider to be among the finest of the world.

In addition to their incomparable Chardonnays, Grgich Hills produces a lush and firm Cabernet Sauvignon from estate vineyards in Yountville as well as a delightfully clean and fruity Fumæ Blanc from their Olive Hills estate vineyard. Of particular interest are their dry-land farmed Zinfandels, grown on hot and windy hillside vineyard sites. These massive wines have impressive fruit and longevity.

RIGATONI
with Ratatouille

This is an excellent dish to use the abundance of a summer garden.

¹/₂ cup olive oil, divided

1 onion, thinly sliced

2 cloves garlic, minced

1 zucchini, cut into thick matchsticks

1 red bell pepper, cut into thick matchsticks

1 eggplant, peeled and cut into thick matchsticks

2¹/₂ cups tomato sauce

¹/₄ cup Grgich Hills Cellar Zinfandel

¹/₄ cup chopped fresh basil

¹/₄ cup chopped fresh parsley

Salt and freshly ground black pepper to taste

1 pound rigatoni, cooked in boiling salted water
   until al dente, then drained

Freshly grated Parmesan cheese

In a skillet, heat 1 tablespoon of the olive oil over medium heat. Ad the onion and garlic and sauté until very tender. Transfer to a large saucepan. Add 1 tablespoon of the olive oil to the skillet and, when hot, add the zucchini and sauté until tender and lightly browned. Transfer the zucchini to the saucepan. Add 1 tablespoon of the olive oil to the skillet and, when hot, add the red bell pepper and sauté until tender and lightly browned. Transfer the red pepper to the saucepan. Add the remaining olive oil to the skillet and, when hot, add the eggplant and sauté until tender and lightly browned. Transfer eggplant to the saucepan. Place the saucepan over medium heat and stir in the tomato sauce, wine, basil, parsley, salt, and pepper and bring to a simmer. Reduce heat to medium-low, cover, and simmer for about 30 minutes, stirring occasionally, until the flavors marry and the sauce has slightly thickened. Divide hot pasta into 6 shallow bowls and top with the ratatouille. Sprinkle with Parmesan and serve immediately.

Serves 6
Serve with Grgich Hills Cellar
Zinfandel

HANDLEY CELLARS

Known as much for her exquisite sparkling wines as her superbly crafted still wines, Milla Handley practices her craft at the cellars she and her husband Rex McClellan founded in 1975. Set in the Northwest end of the Anderson Valley, protected to the west by redwood covered coastal ridges and to the east by oak studded hills, Handley Cellars is situated in a unique viticultural region. The Mendocino appellation, by virtue of its cool foggy nights and gentle summers, is ideally suited to the production of aromatic and delicate whites, luscious and elegant reds, and crisp and flavorful sparklers.

LINGUINE *with* Vodka & Spicy Yellow Tomato Sauce

Your guests won't begin to imagine that the bright flavors are from tomatoes!

2 tablespoons butter

2 tablespoons olive oil

$1/2$ cup finely chopped onion

3 cloves garlic, minced

$1/2$ teaspoon dried red chile flakes

$1/4$ cup vodka

1 pound 12 ounces yellow tomatoes, peeled, seeded, and chopped

$1/2$ cup heavy cream

2 tablespoons finely chopped fresh basil

Salt and freshly white ground pepper to taste

12 ounces linguine, cooked in boiling salted water until al dente, then drained

 In a skillet, melt butter and olive oil together over medium heat. Add the onion, garlic, and chile flakes and sauté until the onion is very tender. Stir in the vodka and simmer until the liquid has almost evaporated. Stir in the tomatoes and simmer until they start to break down. Stir in the cream and

(recipe continued on next page)

simmer until the sauce is slightly thickened.
Stir in the basil. Season with salt and white pepper.
Gently stir in the hot pasta until coated. Serve
immediately.

Serves 4
Serve with Handley Cellars
Pinot Noir

Bring water, bring wine, boy!
Bring flower garlands to me!
Yes, bring them,
so that I may try a bout with love.

Anacreon

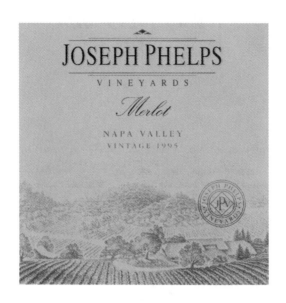

JOSEPH PHELPS
VINEYARDS

Few wineries in Northern California have more "firsts" to their name than the winery of Joseph Phelps. "Insignia," the first Bordeaux-style blend to be produced in California as a proprietary wine ushered in the era of the "Meritage" wines. His 1974 Syrah was perhaps the first time that variety had been bottled as such. And since 1990, his Vin du Mistral wines have epitomized the classic Rhone varietals.

Located in a stunning, redwood building, the winery is anchored to the landscape by a massive wisteria-covered trellis made from 100-year-old recycled bridge timbers. It is definitely worth an appointment to visit this pioneer of the modern Napa Valley.

RISOTTO *with* Gorgonzola

This would be a great side dish to a meal of either pot roast, braised beef ribs, or Osso Bucco, Italy's slow-braised veal shanks.

4 ounces Gorgonzola cheese

2 tablespoons heavy cream

$1/3$ cup butter

1 cup finely chopped red onion

2 cups arborio rice

6 cups low-sodium beef stock

Freshly ground black pepper to taste

Minced Italian parsley, for garnish

Crumble the Gorgonzola into a small bowl. Add the cream and mash together with a fork. Set aside.

In a large saucepan, heat butter over medium heat. Add red onion and sauté until translucent. Stir in rice and sauté until it is just translucent around the edges. In a saucepan, bring the beef stock to a simmer over medium heat. Ladle enough simmering stock into the rice to just cover it. Stir constantly until rice has almost absorbed all of the liquid. Add more simmering stock to just cover the rice and continue stirring until almost absorbed. Repeat this process until the rice is tender but still firm. This will take about 20 minutes. Take the saucepan off of the heat and stir in the reserved Gorgonzola mixture until it has melted and the risotto is creamy. Season with pepper to taste. Sprinkle with parsley and serve immediately.

Serves 6
Serve with Joseph Phelps Vineyards
Merlot

KENWOOD VINEYARDS

At Kenwood Vineyards each vineyard lot is handled separately within the winery to preserve its individuality. Such "small lot" winemaking allows the winemaker to bring each lot of wine to its fullest potential. This style of winemaking is evident in the quality of Kenwood's special bottlings. From the Jack London Vineyard series, whose grapes come from the historical lava-terraced vineyards of the Jack London Ranch, to the Artist Series Cabernet Sauvignon, whose labels each year feature the work of a renowned artist, Kenwood's reds show Sonoma at its best.

HERBED LINGUINE
and Yellow Peppers with Grilled Steak

The talented and original Linda Kittler created this delicious make-in-advance summer dish.

VINAIGRETTE:

$^1/_2$ cup olive oil

$^1/_3$ cup balsamic vinegar

$^1/_4$ cup minced shallots

$^1/_4$ cup chopped fresh basil

2 tablespoons capers, chopped

2 tablespoons Dijon mustard

2 tablespoons minced garlic

2 tablespoons red wine vinegar

2 teaspoons marjoram

2 teaspoons thyme

1 teaspoon freshly ground black pepper to taste

1 teaspoon coarse salt

1 pound linguine, cooked in boiling salted water
until al dente, then drained

6 yellow bell peppers

$^1/_4$ cup olive oil

6 New York steaks

3 tablespoons olive oil

Salt and freshly ground black pepper to taste

(recipe continued on next page)   **65**

 **For the vinaigrette:** In a large bowl, whisk together all of the vinaigrette ingredients. Stir in the hot pasta and let cool. Cover and chill overnight.

The following day, take the pasta out of the refrigerator 2 hours before serving and toss occasionally to be sure that the vinaigrette is well incorporated.

Prepare the grill. Cut the tops off the yellow bell peppers and reserve the tops for garnish. Clean out the seeds and ribs. Brush the peppers inside and out with $1/4$ cup olive oil and season the insides with salt and pepper. Grill peppers over hot coals just until the skin is blistered on all sides. Do not overcook or the peppers will not hold their shape.

Rub the steaks with 3 tablespoons olive oil and season with salt and pepper. Grill until desired doneness. To serve, divide the pasta and fill the peppers. Lay the peppers on their side on a plate and let the pasta spill out. Slice the steaks and fan them out on the pasta. Set the reserved pepper tops propped up next to the opening of the pepper. Serve immediately.

Serves 6
Serve with Kenwood Vineyards
Jack London Cabernet Sauvignon

KENDALL-JACKSON
WINERY

In 1974, Jess Jackson and his family purchased an 85-acre pear ranch near Lakeport, in Northern California. By 1982 the ranch was a vineyard, the barn was a tasting room, and the pasture was a winery. Meanwhile, they studied premium vineyards that span California's cool coastal growing regions and discovered the wonderful spectrum of flavors produced by the same grape varietal grown in different locations. Why not use this exciting diversity? Why not blend the best grapes from the best vineyards to produce unique wines with layers of depth and complexity?

Their first Chardonnay was made in 1982 from vineyards in Santa Barbara, Monterey, Sonoma, and Lake Counties. This wine was named "Best American Chardonnay" by the American Wine Competition. Their concept of blending the best with the best was affirmed and to this day continues to be the reason their wines are noted for their consistency and complexity, vintage after vintage.

GREEK BEEF
& ORZO STEW

After a day skiing at one of Northern California's heavenly ski resorts or even after an afternoon shoveling snow in your own backyard, this heart-warming Greek Stew will drive memories of cold far away.

1/4 cup butter

1 onion, chopped

2 pounds stewing beef

2 cloves garlic, minced

1 1/2 teaspoons salt

1 teaspoon freshly ground black pepper to taste

1 teaspoon oregano

1/2 teaspoon sugar

6 tomatoes, peeled, seeded, and chopped

1 cup red wine

1 pound orzo

Freshly grated kefalotiri or Parmesan cheese

Preheat oven to 350°F.

In a large pot, melt butter over medium heat. Add onion and sauté until translucent. Add beef, garlic, salt, pepper, oregano, sugar, tomatoes, and wine and stir to mix. Cover pot and bake for about 2 hours or until meat is very tender. Stir every 30 minutes, and add water if stew gets too dry.

Stir in orzo, making sure that it is evenly distributed. Cover and return to oven for an additional 25 to 30 minutes, or until orzo is al dente. The orzo will absorb quite a lot of liquid so stir well after 15 minutes to make sure that the mixture is not sticking to the bottom of the pot and scorching. If it seems too dry, stir in about 1 cup of boiling water. Taste for seasoning, more salt and pepper may be needed. Ladle into bowls and sprinkle with cheese.

Serves 6 to 8
Serve with Kendall-Jackson Winery
Cabernet Sauvignon

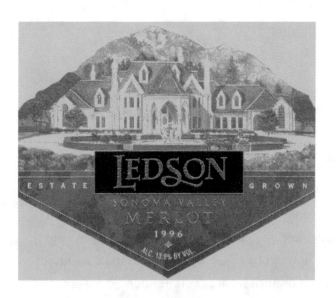

LEDSON VINEYARDS
AND WINERY

One of Northern California's newest wineries, Ledson is rapidly making a name for itself with its reserve Merlots, floral and fruity Rieslings, and intense Chardonnays. Located in Sonoma County's Valley of the Moon, Ledson is at home in a fantastic brick and mortar gothic-style mansion known affectionately as "The Castle." Two full-time chefs guarantee Ledson's commitment to the art and culture of pairing food and great wine.

SPINACH GNOCCHI
with Fontina Cream Sauce

Its hard to say which will steal the show, these delicate, yet beguiling gnocchi or the Ledson Merlot. Either way, this is a dish guaranteed to impress and please.

SPINACH GNOCCHI:

2 pounds russet potatoes

2 teaspoons butter

4 ounces fresh spinach, finely chopped

2 egg yolks

1/2 teaspoon salt

1/4 teaspoon white pepper

3/4 cup all-purpose flour

FONTINA CREAM SAUCE:

14 ounces fontina cheese, diced

1 cup heavy cream

1/2 cup butter

1/4 cup freshly grated Parmesan cheese

Salt and white pepper to taste

(recipe continued on next page)

🪶 **For the gnocchi:** Preheat oven to 400°F.

Scrub the potatoes and prick all over with a fork. Bake for 1 hour. While the potatoes are still hot, cut in half and cool slightly. When cool enough to handle, remove the skin and discard. Put potato through a potato ricer or food mill into a large bowl.

In a nonstick skillet, heat butter over medium heat. Add the spinach and sauté until wilted and all liquid has evaporated. Cool completely.

In a small bowl, whisk together the spinach, egg yolks, salt, and white pepper until well blended. With a wooden spoon, stir mixture into the potatoes until well blended. Stir in the flour until you have a stiff dough. Turn out onto a lightly floured board and knead until smooth, sprinkling with additional flour if the dough sticks. Divide into 5 pieces. Flour your hands and, using the palms of your hands, roll each piece into a log about 1 inch in diameter. Cut the logs into 1-inch pieces. Place them on a lightly floured baking sheet so that they do not touch.

Bring a large pot of salted water to a boil. Add the gnocchi and cook until they float to the surface. With a slotted spoon, transfer the gnocchi to a colander and drain well.

For the sauce: In the top of a double boiler, combine fontina, cream, butter, and Parmesan. Cook over simmering water, stirring often, until melted. Season with salt and white pepper. Divide the gnocchi into 6 shallow bowls and spoon sauce over.

Serves 6
Serve with Ledson
Merlot

Wel loved he garleek,
onyons and lekes,
And for to drynken strong wyn,
reed as blood.

Chaucer

PINOT NOIR
RUSSIAN RIVER VALLEY
VINTAGE 1996

MARK WEST ESTATE
VINEYARD AND WINERY

Certified organic since 1990, Mark West Estate Vineyard and Winery is located where the cooling effects of the nearby Pacific Ocean and the fogs of San Pablo Bay provide ideal growing conditions for their fruit. Their 66 acres of Chardonnay, Pinot Noir, Gewürztraminer, and Merlot, whose original plantings date back to 1974, show restrained elegance and delicate, yet multilayered fruit. Ideal to show off the nuances of a subtly seasoned cuisine, the wines of Mark West are proof positive that wine enhances a fine meal.

BUTTERNUT SQUASH RAVIOLI
with Sage Butter Sauce

The enchanting Barbara Hom combined the flavors of autumn squash, a hint of ginger, and the seduction of Pinot Noir to come up with these amazing ravioli. Prepare in advance for a stress-free dinner party.

BUTTERNUT SQUASH RAVIOLI:

1 butternut squash (approximately 2 pounds)

Salt and freshly ground black pepper to taste

1/4 cup olive oil

1 egg

3 tablespoons heavy cream

1 teaspoon finely minced ginger

1/2 teaspoon freshly grated nutmeg

1 package wonton skins

1 egg, lightly beaten for an egg wash

SAGE BUTTER SAUCE:

6 tablespoons cold butter, divided

2 tablespoons minced shallots

1/4 cup Mark West Estate Vineyard and Winery Pinot Noir

1 tablespoon minced fresh sage

(recipe continued on next page)

🍂 Preheat the oven to 350°F. Oil a baking pan just large enough to hold the squash.

For the ravioli: Slice the squash lengthwise and scoop out the seeds. Cut the squash into 1-inch slices. Place in prepared baking pan and season well with salt and pepper. Pour olive oil over the squash and toss to coat. Roast in the oven for 45 minutes. Remove from oven and let cool. When cool enough to handle, peel off the skin and discard. In the bowl of a food processor, combine squash, 1 egg, cream, ginger, and nutmeg. Process until smooth. Taste for seasoning and add salt and pepper if needed.

Place a wonton skin on a work surface and brush lightly with beaten egg. Place 2 teaspoons of filling in the center. Top with another wonton skin and seal the edges together. Lightly sprinkle a baking sheet with flour. Place ravioli on baking sheet so that they are not touching each other. Continue until all filling is used.

For the sage butter sauce: In a small saucepan, melt 1 tablespoon of butter over medium heat. Add the shallots and sauté until tender. Stir in wine and simmer until the liquid is reduced by half. Take saucepan off the heat and whisk in the remaining butter, 1 tablespoon at a time, until all is incorporated. Stir in the sage and keep barely warm. Do not let the sauce get too hot or it will separate.

Bring a large pot of salted water to a boil. Add the ravioli and cook until they rise to the surface, about 4 minutes. Drain and divide ravioli onto 6 plates. Top with the sage butter sauce and serve immediately.

Serves 6
Serve with Mark West Estate Vineyard and Winery Pinot Noir

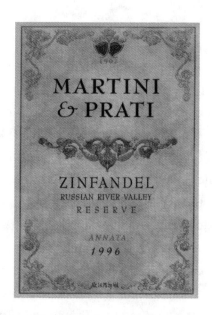

MARTINI AND PRATI
WINERY

One of the oldest family-owned wineries in California,
Martini and Prati's history goes back to the turn of the
century when Rafael Martini settled in the Russian
River Valley north of Sebastopol. A winegrower from
Italy, Rafael Martini quickly felt at home in Sonoma
County, whose gentle climate and rolling hills reminded
him of his native Tuscany. He purchased the Twin Fir
Winery which had been built in 1881, renamed it the R.
Martini Wine Company, and began a tradition that
still exists today.

WILD MUSHROOM & GOAT CHEESE RAVIOLI *with* Fresh Tomato Sauce

Chef Barbara Hom pulled no flavor punches in creating this amazing dish of wild mushroom and chèvre for the Martini and Prati Winery.

WILD MUSHROOM AND GOAT CHEESE RAVIOLI:

3 tablespoons olive oil

2 cups chopped assorted wild mushrooms such as chanterelles, porcini, and shiitake

4 cloves garlic, minced

2 cups chopped Swiss chard

11 ounces goat cheese, crumbled

2 eggs, lightly beaten

1 tablespoon minced fresh marjoram

Salt and freshly ground black pepper to taste

20 (6-inch square) egg roll wrappers

1 egg

1 tablespoon water

(recipe continued on next page)

FRESH TOMATO SAUCE:

3 tablespoons olive oil

4 cloves garlic, minced

12 Roma tomatoes, coarsely chopped

$1/4$ cup thinly sliced fresh basil

❧ **For the ravioli:** In a large skillet, heat olive oil over medium heat. Add mushrooms and garlic and sauté until tender. Add chard and sauté until tender and liquid has evaporated. Remove from heat and cool completely. In a bowl, blend goat cheese and 2 eggs with a fork until smooth. Stir in cooled mushroom mixture and marjoram. Season well with salt and pepper.

Cut each egg roll wrapper in half into two (3 x 6-inch) rectangles. In a small bowl, whisk together 1 egg and water to make an egg wash. Place a rectangle on a work surface and brush lightly with egg wash. Place a tablespoon of filling in the center. Fold in half and seal the edges to make a (3 x 3-inch) ravioli. Place on a lightly floured baking sheet. Continue until filling and wrappers are used.

Bring a large pot of salted water to a boil. Add ravioli and cook until they rise to the surface. Drain and divide onto plates.

For the sauce: In a large skillet, heat olive oil over medium-high heat. Add garlic and sauté just until fragrant. Add tomatoes and sauté until just tender. Stir in basil and heat through. Serve immediately over ravioli.

Serves 6 to 8
Serve with Martini and Prati Winery
Reserve Zinfandel

Worries enough come all the time,
And the cure therefore
is the beloved vine.
Johann Wolfgang von Goethe

MONT ST. JOHN CELLARS

A respect for the land and family traditions are traits that characterize owner and winemaker Andrea "Buck" Bartolucci. One of the first to recognize the uniqueness of the Carneros district, Buck and his father Louis, purchased and planted 160 acres to Pinot Noir and Chardonnay. Following early success with their grapes, Buck and Louis purchased a small plot of land in 1977 near their vineyards and started Mont St. John Cellars.

Buck, as president and winemaker, believes that the vineyard should always dictate the style of the wine. Although he has a degree in enology and viticulture, he considers himself a caretaker, rather than a viticulturist. His convictions individualize Buck Bartolucci and enable him to create quality wines.

FETTUCCINE *with Roasted Red Peppers, Mushrooms & Artichokes*

This is a great harvest lunch, served with bowls of tossed salad, crusty French bread, and bottles of Mont St. John Cabernet Sauvignon.

4 red bell peppers

1/4 cup olive oil, divided

1 onion, chopped

3 cloves garlic, minced

8 ounces mushroom, quartered

1 cup Mont St. John Cellars Cabernet Sauvignon

1 pound Roma tomatoes, peeled, seeded, and chopped

1 can (14-ounces) water-packed artichoke bottoms, diced

3 tablespoons capers

1 teaspoon thyme

1/4 teaspoon dried red chile flakes

Salt and freshly ground black pepper to taste

12 ounces fettuccine, cooked in boiling salted water until al dente, then drained

Freshly grated Parmesan cheese

(recipe continued on next page)

❧ Preheat oven to 450°F. Lightly oil a baking sheet. Brush the bell peppers with 2 tablespoons of the olive oil and place on the prepared baking sheet. Roast the peppers for about 30 minutes or until blackened. Remove from oven and place hot peppers in plastic bag. Let them steam in the bag until cool. Remove the skins and discard. Thinly slice the peppers and set aside.

In a skillet, heat the remaining 2 tablespoons of olive oil over medium heat. Add the onion and garlic and sauté until translucent. Add the mushrooms and sauté until tender. Stir in the wine and bring to a simmer. Stir in reserved roasted red peppers, tomatoes, artichokes, capers, thyme, and chile flakes and bring to a simmer. Reduce heat to medium-low, cover, and simmer 20 minutes. Season to taste with salt and pepper. Divide pasta onto 4 plates and spoon sauce over. Sprinkle with Parmesan and serve immediately.

Serves 4
Serve with Mont St. John Cellars
Cabernet Sauvignon

QUAIL RIDGE CELLARS
AND VINEYARDS

Quail Ridge Cellars and Vineyards, Napa Valley's rustic gem, is nestled snugly in mid–Napa Valley. Quail Ridge's comfortable setting provides a welcome respite from the crowded surroundings of larger Napa wineries. Quail Ridge produces a number of excellent varietals that have won numerous medals in international wine competitions.

Located off Highway 29 on a 9-acre vineyard in the town of Rutherford, Quail Ridge is an integral part of the storied Rutherford Bench growing region. From its redwood deck, it is possible to enjoy the beauty and grandeur of the majestic Mayacamas mountain range, the historical divider of Napa and Sonoma Counties.

TAGLIATELLE *with* *Ham, Smoked Salmon, & Caviar*

It doesn't always have to be Beluga. Simple lumpfish caviar will do just fine in this quick-to-prepare pasta dish.

1/4 cup butter

1 tablespoon minced fresh sage

8 ounces ham, cut into 1/2-inch cubes

5 ounces smoked salmon, cut into 1/2-inch cubes

1 cup heavy cream

1/8 teaspoon freshly grated nutmeg

Salt and freshly ground black pepper to taste

12 ounces tagliatelle pasta, cooked in boiling salted
water until al dente, then drained

2 tablespoons freshly grated Parmesan cheese

2 tablespoons black caviar

In a saucepan, melt the butter over medium heat. Add the sage and sauté until fragrant. Add the ham and sauté until lightly browned. Add the salmon and heat through. Stir in the cream and just bring to a simmer. Stir in the nutmeg, salt and pepper. Add the hot pasta and toss to coat. Divide onto 4 plates and sprinkle with Parmesan. Top with caviar and serve immediately.

Serves 4
Serve with Quail Ridge Cellars and Vineyards Merlot

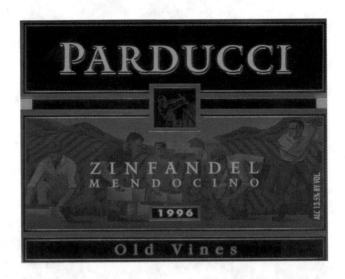

PARDUCCI WINE ESTATES

There are only two things you need to know about a wine. First, do you like it? Second, can you afford it? The people at Parducci are confident that, after tasting and pricing Parducci Wines, the answer to both questions will be an emphatic "YES."

They have always recognized that wine customers enjoy a variety of wines. As such, they have taken advantage of the numerous varieties grown in Mendocino County and produce the following wines: Cabernet Sauvignon, Chenin Blanc, Pinot Noir, Chardonnay, Charbono, Barbera, Petite Sirah, Merlot, Sauvignon Blanc, Zinfandel, Syrah, and Sangiovese. Parducci strives to bring out the varietal characteristics each grape has to offer. Wine is an honest, natural product that should never be over-processed. It should have a softness that invites pleasant consumption upon release.

SPAGHETTI DELL UBRIACONE
(Drunken Spaghetti)

My dear friend Patricia Caringella brought this simple but delicious first course recipe home from a small trattoria in Florence. It is a taste of heaven when served with the Parducci Zinfandel.

3 tablespoons butter

3 tablespoons olive oil

1 teaspoon minced garlic

1/4 cup finely chopped Italian parsley

1 cup Parducci Wine Estates Zinfandel

Salt and freshly ground black pepper to taste

12 ounces spaghetti, cooked in boiling salted water until al dente, then drained

 In a skillet, heat butter and olive oil together over medium heat. Add garlic and sauté until fragrant. Add parsley and wine and simmer until liquid is reduced by half. Season well with salt and pepper. Stir in hot spaghetti and simmer, stirring gently until the liquid is absorbed by the pasta. Serve immediately.

> *Serves 6*
> *Serve with Parducci Wine Estates Zinfandel*

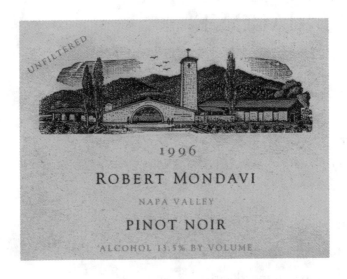

1996

ROBERT MONDAVI

NAPA VALLEY

PINOT NOIR

ALCOHOL 13.5% BY VOLUME

ROBERT MONDAVI WINERY

Founded in 1966 by Robert Mondavi and his son, Michael, the Robert Mondavi Winery is considered a leader in the modern wine industry. They are committed to producing naturally balanced wines of great finesse and elegance, which complement and enhance fine food. They have been successful in achieving these goals through Earth-friendly farming practices, a sophisticated winery emphasizing gentle treatment of their wines, and a genuine love for their handiwork. No other winery epitomizes the Napa Valley like the Robert Mondavi Winery.

LAMB RAVIOLI *with* Prosciutto Cream Sauce

These ravioli can be served as a light lunch by themselves, or as the first course at an elegant dinner party.

LAMB RAVIOLI:

2 tablespoons olive oil

2 shallots, finely minced

2 cloves garlic, finely minced

1 carrot, minced

1 rib celery, minced

1 pound ground lamb

1/4 cup Robert Mondavi Winery Pinot Noir

2 cups veal stock

Salt and freshly ground pepper to taste

20 (6-inch square) egg roll wrappers

1 egg

1 teaspoon water

PROSCIUTTO CREAM SAUCE:

1 teaspoon butter

4 ounces prosciutto, minced

3 cups heavy cream

Salt and white pepper to taste

Thinly sliced fresh basil, for garnish

(recipe continued on next page)

❧ **For the ravioli:** In a skillet, heat olive oil over medium heat. Add the shallots and garlic and sauté until tender. Add the carrot and celery and sauté until very tender. Add the lamb and sauté until lightly browned. Make sure that the lamb is completely crumbled. Stir in the wine and simmer for 5 minutes. Stir in the stock and bring to a simmer. Reduce heat to medium-low and simmer until the liquid has evaporated. Remove from heat and cool completely. Season well with salt and pepper.

Cut each egg roll wrapper in half into two (3 x 6-inch) rectangles. In a small bowl, whisk together the egg and water to make an egg wash. Place a rectangle on a work surface and brush lightly with egg wash. Place a tablespoon of filling in the center. Fold in half and seal the edges to make a (3 x 3-inch) square ravioli. Place on a lightly floured baking sheet so that they do not touch. Continue until filling and wrappers are used. Set aside.

For the prosciutto cream sauce: In a saucepan, melt butter over medium heat. Add the prosciutto and sauté until lightly crisped. Stir in the cream and simmer until mixture is reduced by half. Season with salt and white pepper.

Bring a large pot of salted water to a boil. Add the ravioli and cook until they rise to the surface. Drain and divide into 6 shallow bowls. Spoon the sauce over the ravioli. Sprinkle with basil and serve immediately.

Serves 6
Serve with Robert Mondavi Winery
Pinot Noir

*I rather like bad wine...
one gets so bored with good wine.*

Disraeli

RODNEY STRONG
VINEYARDS

Over 35 years ago, Rodney Strong was one of the first to recognize Sonoma County's potential for excellence. After searching for vineyard land that would bring each grape variety to its fullest potential, Rodney Strong finally selected vineyard sites in the Chalk Hill, Alexander Valley, and Russian River Valley appellations to produce his wine. In the cellar, he employs the subtle use of barrel and stainless steel fermentation, oak aging, and other winemaking techniques to bring out the best in the fruit. That is in keeping with his philosophy to allow the grapes from each vineyard to express their individual character in the final bottled wine.

SPAGHETTI
with Walnut Pesto

*Most are familiar with pesto with pinenuts;
this version with walnuts is superb.*

1 cup shelled walnuts

1 cup packed fresh basil leaves

$^1/_2$ cup freshly grated Parmesan cheese

1 teaspoon minced garlic

Salt and freshly ground black pepper to taste

$^1/_2$ cup olive oil

1 pound spaghetti, cooked in boiling salted water
    until al dente, then drained

Preheat oven to 350°F.

Spread the walnuts on a baking sheet. Toast in
the oven for about 7 minutes, shaking the pan occasionally. Let the walnuts cool completely.

In the bowl of a food processor, combine the walnuts, basil, Parmesan, garlic, salt, and pepper. Pulse,
scraping down sides often, until mixture is ground to
a coarse paste. With the motor running, add the olive
oil in a thin stream. Mixture will be creamy. Toss the
hot pasta with the pesto and serve immediately.

*Serves 6
Serve with Rodney Strong Vineyards
Russian River Valley Pinot Noir*

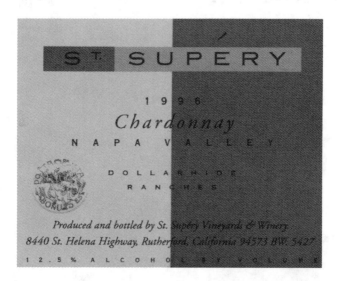

ST. SUPÉRY VINEYARDS AND WINERY

No visit to the Napa Valley would be complete without a visit to the St. Supéry Wine Discovery Center in Rutherford. A demonstration vineyard, it has galleries filled with panoramic murals and displays that illustrate the lore of the vine. Both self-guided as well as guided tours introduce the visitor to the wines and philosophy of St. Supéry.

LIGHTENING BEEF & MUSHROOMS
with Spaghetti

*Chef Sunny Cristadoro devised this quick
and healthful dish that is low in fat and
high in flavor.*

1/2 cup St. Supéry Vineyards and Winery Cabernet
   Sauvignon

2 tablespoons tomato paste

1 tablespoon plus 1 teaspoon Worcestershire sauce

2 teaspoons thyme

1/2 teaspoon freshly ground black pepper to taste

1/2 teaspoon Tabasco sauce

1 tablespoon olive oil

1 tablespoon minced garlic

1 tablespoon minced orange zest

12 ounces flank steak, thinly sliced against the grain

1 pound mushrooms, sliced

4 carrots, grated

1/3 cup chopped fresh parsley

12 ounces spaghetti, cooked in boiling salted water
   until al dente, then drained

(recipe continued on next page)

In a bowl, whisk together wine, tomato paste, Worcestershire sauce, thyme, pepper, and Tabasco sauce until blended. Set aside.

In a large skillet, heat the olive oil over medium-high heat. Add the garlic and orange zest and sauté until just fragrant. Add the beef and sauté until cooked rare. Transfer beef to a bowl. To the skillet, add the mushrooms and sauté until tender. Add carrots, parsley, and reserved sauce and bring to a simmer. Return beef to the skillet and add the spaghetti. Stir gently until the sauce has thickened slightly. Serve immediately.

Serves 6
Serve with St. Supéry
Cabernet Sauvignon

SEAVEY VINEYARD

More than 120 years ago, the vineyards the Seaveys now culti-
vate were planted with grapes to make "claret of high repute,"
judged by the St. Helena Star *of that day to be "as fine as one*
might find anywhere." This was back when Conn Valley Road
was little more than a wagon trail and the label of the wine was
"Franco-Swiss Cellar" under the ownership of G. Crochat &
Co. After the breakup of the company in the early 1900s, no more
grapes were grown on the property until Bill and Mary Seavey
acquired it and began to replant the vineyards in 1981, with
Chardonnay in the cooler areas along Conn Creek, and Caber-
net Sauvignon on the adjoining south-facing hillsides. In 1986,
the Seaveys acquired land above their property and added small
blocs of Merlot, Cabernet Franc, and Petite Verdot as well as
more Cabernet Sauvignon for a current total of 38 acres of vine-
yard. In 1990, they completed renovation of the 1881 stone barn
as their small winery, and began selecting grapes for limited lots
of estate-produced Cabernet Sauvignon and Chardonnay.

PORTOBELLO MUSHROOMS
& *Fettuccine*

This simple-to-prepare dish combines two naturals, portobello mushrooms and Seavey Vineyard Merlot, for a delicious and quick meal.

$^1/_3$ cup olive oil

1 onion, thinly sliced

2 cloves garlic, minced

4 large portobello mushrooms, cut into $^1/_2$-inch slices

$1^1/_2$ teaspoons Worcestershire sauce

$^1/_2$ teaspoon dry mustard

$^1/_4$ cup Seavey Vineyard Merlot

$^1/_2$ cup sour cream

Salt and freshly ground black pepper to taste

12 ounces fettuccine, cooked in boiling salted water until al dente, then drained

In a large skillet, heat the olive oil over medium-high heat, Add the onion and garlic and sauté until tender. Add the mushrooms and sauté until just tender; do not overcook or mushrooms will lose their meaty texture. Reduce heat to medium and stir in Worcestershire sauce and mustard. Stir in the wine and simmer for about 3 minutes, or until slightly reduced. Stir in sour cream and simmer until heated through. Season with salt and pepper. Divide hot pasta onto 4 plates and top with mushrooms.

Serves 4
Serve with Seavey Vineyard
Merlot

Wine that maketh glad the heart of man.

The Bible

SHAFER VINEYARDS

Located in the heart of the Stags Leap District of the Napa Valley, Shafer Vineyards has become synonymous with the finest the Napa Valley has to offer. Since their first crush in 1978, John Shafer and his son Doug have presided over the slow but steady growth of their premium winery from an initial 1000-case production to its present size. Highly acclaimed by colleagues within the wine industry, the wines from Shafer Vineyards reflect their "terroir" through their complex spectrum of aromas and flavors.

RICOTTA RAVIOLI
with Marinara

Homemade ravioli are a special treat, and the egg roll wrappers make the assembly so much easier.

MARINARA SAUCE:

1/3 cup olive oil

6 cloves garlic, minced

2 onions, finely chopped

1 carrot, finely chopped

1/2 cup green bell pepper, finely chopped

8 tomatoes, peeled, seeded and chopped

1 can (1 pound, 13 ounces) tomato sauce

1 can (12 ounces) tomato paste

2 teaspoons oregano

2 teaspoons salt

1 teaspoon basil

1 teaspoon thyme

1/2 teaspoon freshly ground black pepper

1/2 cup to 1 cup Shafer Vineyards Merlot

(recipe continued on next page)

RICOTTA RAVIOLI:

1 pound ricotta cheese

1 ounce Parmesan cheese, freshly grated

$1/2$ teaspoon minced garlic

$1/2$ teaspoon salt

$1/4$ teaspoon freshly ground black pepper to taste

3 egg yolks

4 ounces mozzarella cheese, freshly grated

2 tablespoons minced scallions

1 teaspoon minced fresh Italian parsley

20 (6-inch square) egg roll wrappers

1 egg

1 teaspoon water

For the marinara sauce: In a large pot, heat olive oil over medium heat. Add garlic and sauté until fragrant. Add onions, carrot, and green pepper and sauté until tender. Add tomatoes and stir until they start to break down. Add tomato sauce, tomato paste, oregano, salt, basil, thyme, black pepper, and wine and stir well. Bring to a simmer, then reduce heat to medium-low, cover, and simmer about 45 minutes, stirring often. If sauce gets too thick, add up to another $1/2$ cup wine. Uncover and simmer about 30 additional minutes, or until flavors meld and sauce is the desired consistency.

For the ricotta ravioli: In a large bowl, beat together ricotta, Parmesan, garlic, salt, and pepper until smooth. Add egg yolks, one at a time, beating well after each addition. Stir in mozzarella, scallions, and parsley until well blended.

Cut each egg roll wrapper in half into two (3 x 6-inch) rectangles. In a small bowl, whisk together egg and water to make an egg wash. Place a rectangle on a lightly floured work surface and brush lightly with egg wash. Place a tablespoon of filling in the center. Fold in half and seal the edges to make a (3 x 3-inch) ravioli. Place on a lightly floured baking sheet. Continue until filling and wrappers are used.

Bring a large pot of salted water to a boil. Add ravioli and cook until they rise to the surface. Drain well and divide onto plates. Top with marinara sauce and serve immediately.

Serves 6 to 8
Serve with Shafer Vineyards
Merlot

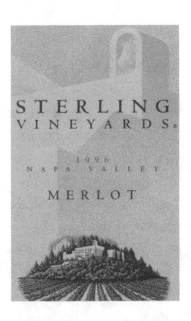

STERLING VINEYARDS

Built in the architectural style of the Greek Island of Mykonos, the Sterling Vineyards winery sits dramatically on top of a 300-foot knoll just south of Napa Valley's northernmost town, Calistoga. Its white, monastic buildings contrast sharply with the dark green of the trees that cover the knoll. Visitors are carried up to the winery by aerial tramway and treated to a spectacular view of the Napa Valley below, as well as a close-up look at the Napa Valley's most dramatic and recognizable winery. The panorama is awe-inspiring and peaceful, punctuated only by the peal of Sterling's antique English bells.

TAGLIATELLE
with Bolognese Sauce

This is the best Bolognese sauce that I have ever made. The secret to this fabulous sauce from Patricia Caringella is to cook it very slowly over low heat; it is worth every minute.

1/4 cup butter

1 onion, finely chopped

1 carrot, finely chopped

1 stalk celery, finely chopped

4 ounces ground beef

4 ounces ground pork

4 ounces ground veal

2 ounces proscuitto ham, finely chopped

1/2 cup white wine

Salt and freshly ground black pepper to taste

1 cup half-and-half

1/4 teaspoon freshly grated nutmeg

1 can (28-ounces) Italian tomatoes with their juice, chopped

1 pound fresh tagliatelle, cooked in boiling salted water until al dente, then drained

Freshly grated Parmesan cheese

(recipe continued on next page)

In a large pot, melt butter over medium-low heat. Add onion, carrot, and celery and sauté until tender. Do not let vegetables brown. Add beef, pork, veal, and proscuitto. Break up the meat and sauté until meat is just barely cooked. Do not let the meats brown. Add wine, salt, and pepper. Simmer slowly until liquid is almost evaporated. Stir in half-and-half and nutmeg. Stir in tomatoes and their juice. Bring to a bare simmer over low or medium-low heat. Cover and simmer gently for 4 to 5 hours, stirring often. The sauce will reduce and become very thick.

Serve over tagliatelle and sprinkle with Parmesan cheese.

Serves 6
Serve with Sterling Vineyards
Merlot

SUTTER HOME
WINERY

Sutter Home is one of California's enviable success stories. Begun in 1874, the winery passed into the hands of its current family-owners in 1947, when John and Mario Trinchero immigrated from Italy and set down roots in the Napa Valley. Today their children carry on this once mom-and-pop operation.

A milestone occurred in 1972 when, in an effort to make his red Zinfandel more robust, Bob Trinchero drew off some of the free run juice and fermented it as a "white" wine. This pale pink Zinfandel became a favorite at the winery's tasting room, and thus was born white Zinfandel.

Today Sutter Home is known not only for their popular White Zinfandel, but also for their high-quality, affordable varietal wines as well as their line of nonalcoholic wines.

PAPPARDELLE
with Braised Rabbit
& Zinfandel

Slow-cooked rabbit is a natural with the hearty flavors of a great Zinfandel, and Sutter Home's Jeffrey Starr's version is one of the best.

1 rabbit (about 3-pounds), cut into serving pieces

Salt and freshly ground black pepper to taste

Flour for dredging

$1/3$ cup olive oil, divided

2 tablespoons butter

3 yellow onions, sliced $1/4$-inch thick

2 tablespoons water

1 tablespoon caraway seeds

1 tablespoon minced garlic

2 cups chopped Roma tomatoes

2 cups Sutter Home Winery Reserve Zinfandel

1 tablespoon minced fresh basil

1 tablespoon finely minced lemon zest

1 tablespoon paprika

$1^1/2$ teaspoons dried red chile flakes

$1/2$ cup finely chopped Italian parsley

1 pound pappardelle pasta, cooked in boiling salted
     water until al dente, then drained

🍃 Season the rabbit pieces with salt and pepper then dredge lightly in flour. In a large skillet, heat ¹/4 cup of the olive oil over medium heat. Add the rabbit and brown on both sides. Transfer rabbit to a plate and set aside.

In the skillet, add remaining olive oil and butter over medium heat. Add the onions, water, and caraway seeds and sauté until onions are tender. Cover tightly and reduce heat to medium-low. Simmer for about 30 minutes, stirring every 10 minutes and adding a little more water if necessary so onions do not burn, until onions are deep golden brown. Stir in the garlic and sauté until fragrant. Add reserved rabbit, tomatoes, wine, basil, lemon zest, paprika, and chile flakes. Cover tightly and simmer over medium-low heat for about 45 minutes, or until the rabbit is very tender. Add the parsley and season with salt and pepper.

Divide hot pasta into 6 shallow bowls. Top with rabbit and spoon sauce over.

Serves 6
Serve with Sutter Home Winery
Reserve Zinfandel

STONE CREEK
WINERY

Stone Creek Wine Tasting Room is located in Kenwood in the heart of Sonoma County. The building once housed the Los Guilicos School, a historical one-room schoolhouse built in 1890. It was one of the first public schools in the Los Guilicos Valley. The "Old Blue Schoolhouse" has a colorful history and is now the home of Stone Creek Wines.

ORECCHIETTE
with Spinach Pesto

Marc Downie of Catering by Design incorporated
Greek flavors into a classic sauce.

1 cup packed fresh spinach

1/4 cup packed fresh basil

3 cloves garlic

2 tablespoons olive oil

2 ounces feta cheese, crumbled

1/4 cup heavy cream

12 ounces orecchiette pasta, cooked in boiling
    salted water until al dente, then drained

In the bowl of a food processor, combine
spinach, basil, garlic, and olive oil and pulse until
smooth, scraping sides as needed. Add feta and
pulse until smooth. Place mixture in a saucepan
and add cream. Heat over medium heat until feta
has melted. Toss with hot pasta and serve.

> *Serves 4*
> *Serve with Stone Creek Winery*
> *Zinfandel*

STONEGATE WINERY

Steep slopes, shallow stony loam soil, and excellent drainage force the vines in Stonegate's vineyards to compete intensely with each other. The results are clearly visible in the reds from these vineyards. Cabernet Sauvignon, Merlot, and Cabernet Franc exhibit excellent structure, dark color, and long lingering finishes. At their best when paired with a fine meal, the wines are full of nuance and flavor. The Chardonnay, planted at the extreme north end of the Napa Valley in the hillside Bella Vista Vineyard is multilayered and chock full of ripe fruit aromas. Stonegate's Estate Bottled Sauvignon Blanc and Late Harvest Dessert Wine come from the vineyard surrounding the winery.

SPAGHETTI *with* *Sundried Tomato Pesto*

The tang of sundried tomatoes brings out
the fruit in the Cabernet Sauvignon.

10 sundried tomato halves packed in oil, coarsely
   chopped

1/2 cup firmly packed basil leaves

1/4 cup firmly packed Italian parsley leaves

3 cloves garlic, chopped

1/2 teaspoon dried red chile flakes

Salt and freshly ground black pepper to taste

1/4 cup olive oil

12 ounces spaghetti, cooked in boiling salted water
   until al dente, then drained

In the bowl of a food processor, combine the
sundried tomatoes, basil, parsley, garlic, chile
flakes, salt, and pepper. Pulse, scraping down sides
often, until mixture is ground to a coarse paste.
With the motor running, add the olive oil in a thin
stream. Mixture will be creamy. Toss the hot pasta
with the pesto and serve immediately.

> *Serves 4*
> *Serve with Stonegate Winery*
> *Cabernet Sauvignon*

TURNBULL WINE CELLARS

Located just south of world-renowned Oakville in the Napa Valley, Turnbull Wine Cellars produces stunning wines of amazing complexity and depth. Proprietor Patrick O'Dell's well-known red wines include Cabernet Sauvignon, Merlot, and Sangiovese, as well as small amounts of Syrah and Zinfandel. A limited amount of elegant Sauvignon Blanc is a special treat for white wine lovers who visit his tasting room.

PENNE
with Merlot Braised Lamb Shanks

Braising brings out the richness of good lamb shanks, and this recipe by Beverley Wolfe of Turnbull Wine Cellars will have you passing your plate for seconds.

4 lamb shanks

Salt and freshly ground black pepper to taste

3 tablespoons olive oil

1 onion, coarsely chopped

3 ribs celery, chopped

2 carrots, chopped

10 cloves garlic, chopped

2 bay leaves

1 tablespoon minced fresh lavender

1 tablespoon minced fresh oregano

1 tablespoon minced fresh sage

1 tablespoon minced fresh thyme

2 cups Turnbull Wine Cellars Merlot

(recipe continued on next page)

VEGETABLES:

8 small new potatoes, cut in half

1/4 cup olive oil, divided

1 tablespoon minced fresh rosemary

Salt and freshly ground black pepper to taste

8 baby artichokes, cut in half

1 tablespoon minced garlic

1 bulb fennel, thinly sliced

8 ounces crimini mushrooms, quartered

3 ounces pitted dry-cured black olives, coarsely chopped

1 tablespoon minced orange zest

1 pound penne pasta, cooked in boiling salted water until al dente, then drained

Freshly grated Parmesan cheese

Preheat oven to 350°F. Oil a large Dutch oven. Season lamb shanks well with salt and pepper. In a large skillet, heat olive oil over medium-high heat. Add the lamb shanks and brown well on all sides. Remove lamb to a plate. Add onion, celery, carrots, and garlic to skillet and sauté until barely tender. Add bay leaves, lavender, oregano, sage, and thyme. Stir in wine and pour mixture into prepared Dutch oven. Place lamb shanks on top of vegetables and cover tightly. Place in oven and cook for about 2 1/2 hours, turning lamb shanks every 30 minutes, until meat is very tender and falls off the bone. Remove lamb and when cool enough to handle, remove meat and chop coarsely. Strain pan vegetables through a colander and reserve the juices. Discard the solids. Set aside the meat and juices.

For the vegetables: In a baking pan, toss potatoes, 2 tablespoons of the olive oil, rosemary, salt, and pepper until coated. Roast in oven next to lamb for 30 minutes. Remove from oven and set aside.

Steam baby artichokes until very tender. Set aside.

In a large skillet, heat remaining 2 tablespoons olive oil over medium heat. Add garlic and sauté until fragrant. Add fennel, mushrooms, olives, and orange zest and sauté until tender. Stir in reserved meat and juices, roasted potatoes, and steamed artichokes. Simmer until heated through. Serve over pasta and sprinkle with Parmesan.

Serves 6 to 8
Serve with Turnbull Wine Cellars
Merlot

THE WINERIES:

Arrowood Vineyards and Winery
14347 Sonoma Highway
Glen Ellen, CA 95442
707.938.5170

Beaulieu Vineyard
1960 St. Helena Highway
Rutherford, CA 94573
707.963.2411

Belvedere Vineyards and Winery
435 West Dry Creek Road
Healdsburg, CA 95448
707.433.8236

Benziger Family Winery
1883 London Ranch Road
Glen Ellen, CA 95442
707.935.3000

Beringer Vineyards
2000 Main Street
St. Helena, CA 94574
707.963.7115

Cakebread Cellars
8300 St. Helena Highway
Rutherford, CA 94573
707.963.5221

Canyon Road Winery
19550 Geyserville Avenue
Geyserville, CA 95441
707.857.3417

Cardinale Winery
Post Office Box 328
Oakville, CA 94562
707.944.2807

Cedar Mountain Winery
7000 Tesla Road
Livermore, CA 94550
510.373.6694

Chateau Montelena Winery
1429 Tubbs Lane
Calistoga, CA 94515
707.942.5105

De Loach Vineyards
1791 Olivet Road
Santa Rosa, CA 95401
707.526.9111

Dry Creek Vineyard
3770 Lambert Bridge Road
Healdsburg, CA 95448
707.433.1000

Duckhorn Vineyards
1000 Lodi Lane
St. Helena, CA 94574
707.963.7108

Ferrari-Carano Vineyards and Winery
8761 Dry Creek Road
Healdsburg, CA 95448
707.433.6700

Freemark Abbey
Highway 29 at Lodi Lane
St. Helena, CA 94574
707.963.9694

Geyser Peak Winery
22281 Chianti Road
Geyserville, CA 95441
707.857.9463

Glen Ellen Winery
14301 Arnold Drive
Glen Ellen, CA 95442
707.939.6277

Grgich Hills Cellar
1829 St. Helena Highway
Rutherford, CA 94573
707.963.2784

Handley Cellars
3153 Highway 128
Philo, CA 95466
707.895.3876

Joseph Phelps Vineyards
200 Taplin Road
St. Helena, CA 94574
707.963.2745

Kendall-Jackson Winery
5007 Fulton Road
Santa Rosa, CA 95439
707.571.8100

Kenwood Vineyards
9592 Sonoma Highway
Kenwood, CA 95452
707.833.5891

Ledson Winery and Vineyards
7335 Sonoma Highway
Kenwood, CA 95452
707.833.2330

Mark West Estate Winery
7010 Trenton-Healdsburg Road
Forestville, CA 95436
707.544.4813

Martini and Prati Winery
2191 Laguna Road
Santa Rosa, CA 95401
707.823.2404

Mont St. John Cellars
5400 Old Sonoma Road
Napa, CA 94558
707.255.8864

Parducci Wine Estates
501 Parducci Road
Ukiah, CA 95482
707.463.5350

Quail Ridge Cellars and Vineyards
1155 Mee Lane
Rutherford, CA 94573
707.963.9783

Robert Mondavi Winery
7801 St. Helena Highway
Oakville, CA 94562
707.226.1395

Rodney Strong Vineyards
11455 Old Redwood Highway
Healdsburg, CA 95448
707.433.6521

St. Supréy Vineyards and Winery
8440 St. Helena Highway
Rutherford, CA 94573
707.963.4507

Seavey Vineyard
1310 Conn Valley Road
St. Helena, CA 94574
707.963.8339

Shafer Vineyards
6154 Silverado Trail
Napa, CA 94558
707.944.9454

Sterling Vineyards
1111 Dunaweal Lane
Calistoga, CA 94515
707.942.3300

Stone Creek Winery
9380 Sonoma Highway
Kenwood, CA 95452
707.833.4455

Stonegate Winery
183 Dunaweal Lane
Calistoga, CA 94515
707.942.6500

Sutter Home Winery
100 St. Helena Highway, South
St. Helena, CA 94574
707.963.3104

Turnbull Wine Cellars
8210 St. Helena Highway
Oakville, CA 94562
800.887.6285

THE CATERERS:

Patricia Caringella Catering
3418 South Shore Road
Lake Oswego, OR 97034
503.636.2952

Catering by Design
Post Office Box 1866
Glen Ellen, CA 95442
707.935.0390

Knickerbocker's Catering
Post Office Box 143
St. Helena, CA 94574
707.963.9278

Monterey Abalone Company
160 Wharf #2
Monterey, CA 93940
831.646.0350

Night Owl Catering
Post Office Box 226
Sebastapol, CA 95472
707.823.1850

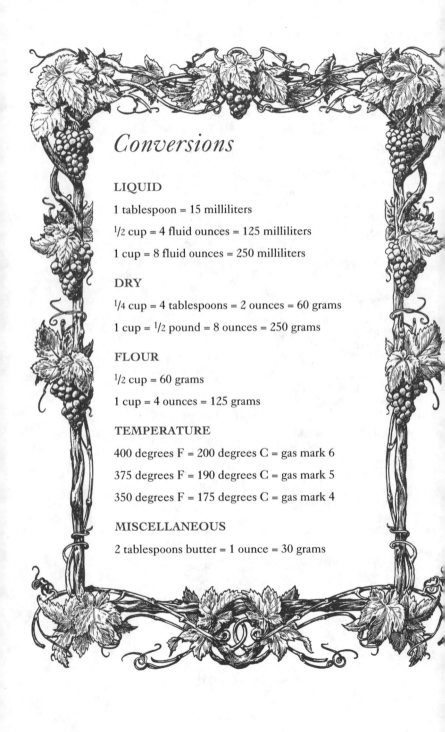

Conversions

LIQUID

1 tablespoon = 15 milliliters

$^1/_2$ cup = 4 fluid ounces = 125 milliliters

1 cup = 8 fluid ounces = 250 milliliters

DRY

$^1/_4$ cup = 4 tablespoons = 2 ounces = 60 grams

1 cup = $^1/_2$ pound = 8 ounces = 250 grams

FLOUR

$^1/_2$ cup = 60 grams

1 cup = 4 ounces = 125 grams

TEMPERATURE

400 degrees F = 200 degrees C = gas mark 6

375 degrees F = 190 degrees C = gas mark 5

350 degrees F = 175 degrees C = gas mark 4

MISCELLANEOUS

2 tablespoons butter = 1 ounce = 30 grams